Creature Classics

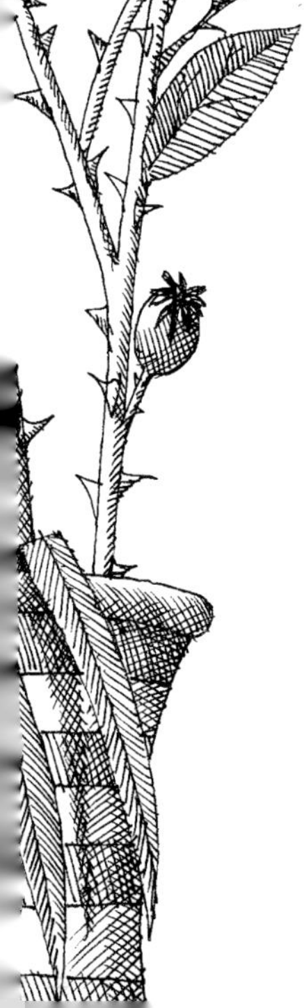

Contents

Creature Classics

E. B. White, Lynne Reid Banks
and Rudyard Kipling

CHARLOTTE'S WEB

by E. B. White

Chapter IV ~ Loneliness

The next day was rainy and dark. Rain fell on the roof of the barn and dripped steadily from the eaves. Rain fell in the barnyard and ran in crooked courses down into the lane where the thistles and pigweed grew. Rain spattered against Mrs Zuckerman's kitchen windows and came gushing out of the downspouts. Rain fell on the backs of the sheep as they grazed in the meadow. When the sheep tired of standing in the rain, they walked slowly up the lane and into the fold.

Rain upset Wilbur's plans. Wilbur had planned to go out, this day, and dig a new hole in his yard. He had other plans, too. His plans for the day went something like this:

Breakfast at six-thirty. Skim milk, crusts, middlings, bits of doughnuts, wheat cakes with drops of maple syrup sticking to them, potato skins, left-over custard pudding with raisins, and bits of Shredded Wheat.

Breakfast would be finished at seven.

From seven to eight, Wilbur planned to have a talk with Templeton, the rat that lived under his trough. Talking with Templeton was not the most interesting occupation in the world but it was better than nothing.

From eight to nine, Wilbur planned to take a nap outdoors in the sun.

From nine to eleven, he planned to dig a hole, or trench, and possibly find something good to eat buried in the dirt.

From eleven to twelve, he planned to stand still and watch flies on the boards, watch bees in the clover, and watch swallows in the air.

Twelve o'clock – lunchtime. Middlings, warm water, apple parings, meat gravy, carrot scrapings, meat scraps, stale hominy and the wrapper off a package of cheese. Lunch would be over at one.

From one to two, Wilbur planned to sleep.

From two to three, he planned to scratch itchy places by rubbing against the fence.

From three to four, he planned to stand perfectly still and think of what it was like to be alive, and to wait for Fern.

At four would come supper. Skim milk, provender, left-over sandwich from Lurvy's lunchbox, prune skins, a morsel of this, a bit of that, fried potatoes, marmalade drippings, a little more of this, a little more of that, a piece of baked apple, a scrap of upside-down cake.

Wilbur had gone to sleep thinking about these plans. He awoke at six and saw the rain, and it seemed as though he couldn't bear it.

"I get everything all beautifully planned out and it has to go and rain," he said.

For a while he stood gloomily indoors. Then he walked to the door and looked out. Drops of rain struck his face. His yard was cold and wet. His trough had an inch of rainwater in it. Templeton was nowhere to be seen.

"Are you out there, Templeton?" called Wilbur. There was no answer. Suddenly Wilbur felt lonely and friendless.

"One day just like another," he groaned. "I'm very young, I have no real friend here in the barn, it's going to rain all morning and all afternoon, and Fern won't come in such bad weather. Oh honestly!" And Wilbur was crying again, for the second time in two days.

At six-thirty Wilbur heard the banging of a pail. Lurvy was standing outside in the rain, stirring up breakfast.

"C'mon, pig!" said Lurvy.

Wilbur did not budge. Lurvy dumped the slops, scraped the pail, and walked away. He noticed that something was wrong with the pig.

Wilbur didn't want food, he wanted love. He wanted a friend – someone who would play with him. He mentioned this to the goose, who was sitting quietly in a corner of the sheepfold.

"Will you come over and play with me?" he asked.

"Sorry, sonny, sorry," said the goose. "I'm sitting-sitting on my eggs. Eight of them. Got to keep them toasty-oasty-oasty warm. I have to stay right here, I'm no flibberty-ibberty-gibbet. I do not play when there are eggs to hatch. I'm expecting goslings."

"Well, I didn't think you were expecting woodpeckers," said Wilbur bitterly.

Wilbur next tried one of the lambs.

"Will you please play with me?" he asked.

"Certainly not," said the lamb. "In the first place,

I cannot get into your pen, as I am not old enough to jump over the fence. In the second place, I am not interested in pigs. Pigs mean less than nothing to me."

"What do you mean, *less* than nothing?" replied Wilbur. "I don't think there is any such thing as *less* than nothing. Nothing is absolutely the limit of nothingness. It's the lowest you can go. It's the end of the line. How can something be less than nothing? If there were something that was less than nothing, then nothing would not be nothing, it would be something – even though it's just a very little bit of something. But if nothing is *nothing*, then nothing has nothing that is less than *it* is."

"Oh, be quiet!" said the lamb. "Go play by yourself! I don't play with pigs."

Sadly, Wilbur lay down and listened to the rain. Soon he saw the rat climbing down a slanting board that he used as a stairway.

"Will you play with me, Templeton?" asked Wilbur.

"Play?" said Templeton, twirling his whiskers. "Play? I hardly know the meaning of the word."

"Well," said Wilbur, "it means to have fun, to frolic, to run and skip and make merry."

"I never do those things if I can avoid them," replied the rat, sourly. "I prefer to spend my time eating, gnawing, spying, and hiding. I am a glutton but not a merrymaker. Right now I am on my way to your trough to eat your breakfast, since you haven't got sense enough to eat it yourself."

And Templeton, the rat, crept stealthily along the wall and disappeared into a private tunnel that he had dug between the door and the trough in Wilbur's yard. Templeton was a crafty rat, and he had things pretty much his own way. The tunnel was an example of his skill and cunning. The tunnel enabled him to get from the barn to his hiding-place under the pig trough without coming out into the open. He had tunnels and runways all over Mr Zuckerman's farm and could get from one place to another without being seen. Usually he slept during the daytime and was abroad only after dark.

Wilbur watched him disappear into his tunnel. In a moment he saw the rat's sharp nose poke out from underneath the wooden trough. Cautiously Templeton pulled himself up over the edge of the trough. This was almost more than Wilbur could stand: on this dreary, rainy day to see his breakfast being eaten by somebody else. He knew Templeton was getting soaked, out there in the pouring rain, but even that didn't comfort him. Friendless, dejected, and hungry, he threw himself down in the manure and sobbed.

Late that afternoon, Lurvy went to Mr Zuckerman. "I think there's something wrong with that pig of yours. He hasn't touched his food."

"Give him two spoonfuls of sulphur and a little molasses," said Mr Zuckerman.

Wilbur couldn't believe what was happening to him when Lurvy caught him and forced the medicine down his throat. This was certainly the worst day of his life. He didn't know whether he could endure the awful loneliness any more.

Darkness settled over everything. Soon there were only shadows and the noises of the sheep chewing their cuds, and occasionally the rattle of a cow-chain up overhead. You can imagine Wilbur's surprise when, out of the darkness, came a small voice he had never heard before. It sounded rather thin, but pleasant. "Do you want a friend, Wilbur?" it said. "I'll be a friend to you. I've watched you all day and I like you."

"But I can't see you," said Wilbur, jumping to his feet. "Where are you? And who are you?"

"I'm right up here," said the voice. "Go to sleep. You'll see me in the morning."

Chapter V ~ Charlotte

The night seemed long. Wilbur's stomach was empty and his mind was full. And when your stomach is empty and your mind is full, it's always hard to sleep.

A dozen times during the night Wilbur woke and stared into the blackness, listening to the sounds and trying to figure out what time it was. A barn is never perfectly quiet. Even at midnight there is usually something stirring.

The first time he woke, he heard Templeton gnawing a hole in the grain bin. Templeton's teeth scraped loudly against the wood and made quite a racket. "That crazy rat!" thought Wilbur. "Why does he have to stay up all night, grinding his clashers and destroying people's property? Why can't he go to sleep, like any decent animal?"

The second time Wilbur woke, he heard the goose turning on her nest and chuckling to herself.

"What time is it?" whispered Wilbur to the goose.

"Probably-obably-obably about half-past eleven," said the goose. "Why aren't you asleep, Wilbur?"

"Too many things on my mind," said Wilbur.

"Well," said the goose, "that's not *my* trouble. I have nothing at all on my mind, but I've too many things under my behind. Have you ever tried to sleep while sitting on eight eggs?"

"No," replied Wilbur. "I suppose it *is* uncomfortable. How long does it take a goose egg to hatch?"

"Approximately-oximately thirty days, all told," answered the goose. "But I cheat a little. On warm afternoons, I just pull a little straw over the eggs and go out for a walk."

Wilbur yawned and went back to sleep. In his dreams he heard again the voice saying, "I'll be a friend to you. Go to sleep – you'll see me in the morning."

About half an hour before dawn, Wilbur woke and listened. The barn was still dark. The sheep lay motionless. Even the goose was quiet. Overhead, on the main floor, nothing stirred: the cows were resting, the horses dozed. Templeton had quit work and gone off somewhere on an errand. The only sound was a slight scraping noise from the rooftop, where the weather-vane swung back and forth. Wilbur loved the barn when it was like this – calm and quiet, waiting for light.

"Day is almost here," he thought.

Through a small window, a faint gleam appeared. One by one the stars went out. Wilbur could see the goose a few feet away. She sat with head tucked under a wing. Then he could see the sheep and the lambs. The sky lightened.

"Oh, beautiful day, it is here at last! Today I shall find my friend."

Wilbur looked everywhere. He searched his pen thoroughly. He examined the window ledge, stared up at the ceiling. But he saw nothing new. Finally he decided he would have to speak up. He hated to break the lovely stillness of dawn by using his voice, but he couldn't think of any other way to locate the mysterious new friend who was nowhere to be seen. So Wilbur cleared his throat.

"Attention, please!" he said in a loud, firm voice. "Will the party who addressed me at bedtime last night kindly make himself or herself known by giving an appropriate sign or signal!"

Wilbur paused and listened. All the other animals lifted their heads and stared at him. Wilbur blushed. But he was determined to get in touch with his unknown friend.

"Attention, please!" he said. "I will repeat the message. Will the party who addressed me at bedtime last night kindly speak up. Please tell me where you are, if you are my friend!"

The sheep looked at each other in disgust.

"Stop your nonsense, Wilbur!" said the oldest sheep. "If you have a new friend here, you are probably disturbing his rest; and the quickest way to spoil a friendship is to wake somebody up in the morning before he is ready. How can you be sure your friend is an early riser?"

"I beg everyone's pardon," whispered Wilbur. "I didn't mean to be objectionable."

He lay down meekly in the manure, facing the door. He did not know it, but his friend was very near. And the old sheep was right – the friend was still asleep.

Soon Lurvy appeared with the slops for breakfast. Wilbur rushed out, ate everything in a hurry, and licked the trough. The sheep moved off down the lane, the gander waddled along behind them, pulling grass. And then, just as Wilbur was settling down for his morning nap, he heard again the thin voice that had addressed him the night before.

"Salutations!" said the voice.

Wilbur jumped to his feet. "Salu-*what*?" he cried.

"Salutations!" repeated the voice.

"What are *they*, and where are *you*?" screamed Wilbur. "Please, *please* tell me where you are. And what are salutations?"

"Salutations are greetings," said the voice. "When I say "salutations", it's just my fancy way of saying hello or good morning. Actually, it's a silly expression, and I am surprised that I used it at all. As for my whereabouts, that's easy! Look up here in the corner of the doorway! Here I am. Look, I'm waving!"

At last Wilbur saw the creature that had spoken to him in such a kindly way. Stretched across the upper part of the doorway was a big spider's web, and hanging from the top of the web, head down, was a large grey spider. She was about the size of a gum-drop. She had eight legs, and she was waving one of them at Wilbur in friendly greeting. "See me now?" she asked.

"Oh, yes indeed," said Wilbur. "Yes indeed! How are you? Good morning! Salutations! Very pleased to meet you. What is your name, please? May I have your name?"

"My name," said the spider, "is Charlotte."

"Charlotte what?" asked Wilbur, eagerly.

"Charlotte A. Cavatica. But just call me Charlotte."

"I think you're beautiful," said Wilbur.

"Well, I *am* pretty," replied Charlotte. "There's no denying that. Almost all spiders are rather nice-looking. I'm not as flashy as some, but I'll do. I wish I could see you, Wilbur, as clearly as you can see me."

"Why can't you?" asked the pig. "I'm right here."

"Yes, but I'm near-sighted," replied Charlotte. "I've always been dreadfully near-sighted. It's good in some ways, not so good in others. Watch me wrap up this fly."

A fly that had been crawling along Wilbur's trough had flown up and blundered into the lower part of Charlotte's web and was tangled in the sticky threads. The fly was beating its wings furiously trying to break loose and free itself.

"First," said Charlotte, "I dive at him." She lunged head first towards the fly. As she dropped, a tiny silken thread unwound from her rear end.

"Next, I wrap him up." She grabbed the fly, threw a few jets of silk round it, and rolled it over and over, wrapping it so that it couldn't move. Wilbur watched in horror. He could hardly believe what he was seeing, and although he detested flies he was sorry for this one.

"There!" said Charlotte. "Now I knock him out, so

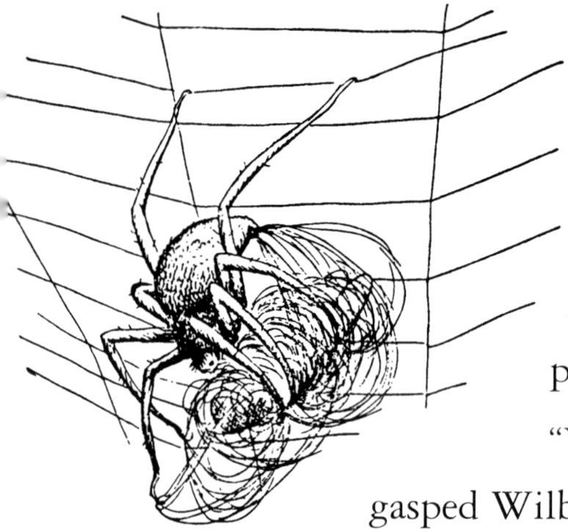

he'll be more comfortable." She bit the fly. "He can't feel a thing now," she remarked. "He'll make a perfect breakfast for me."

"You mean you eat flies?" gasped Wilbur.

"Certainly. Flies, bugs, grasshoppers, choice beetles, moths, butterflies, tasty cockroaches, gnats, midges, daddy-long-legs, centipedes, mosquitoes, crickets – anything that is careless enough to get caught in my web. I have to live, don't I?"

"Why, yes, of course," said Wilbur. "Do they taste good?"

"Delicious. Of course, I don't really eat them. I drink them – drink their blood. I love blood," said Charlotte, and her pleasant, thin voice grew even thinner and more pleasant.

"Don't say that!" groaned Wilbur. "Please don't say things like that!"

"Why not? It's true, and I have to say what is true. I am not entirely happy about my diet of flies and bugs, but it's the way I'm made. A spider has to pick up a living somehow or other, and I happen to be a trapper. I just naturally build a web and trap flies and other insects. My mother was a trapper before me. Her mother was a trapper before her. All our family have been trappers. Way back for thousands and thousands of years we spiders have been laying for flies and bugs."

"It's a miserable inheritance," said Wilbur, gloomily. He was sad because his new friend was so bloodthirsty.

"Yes, it is," agreed Charlotte. "But I can't help it. I don't know how the first spider in the early days of the world happened to think up this fancy idea of spinning a web, but she did, and it was clever of her, too. And since then, all of us spiders have had to work the same trick. It's not a bad pitch on the whole."

"It's cruel," replied Wilbur, who did not intend to be argued out of his position.

"Well, *you* can't talk," said Charlotte. "*You* have your meals brought to you in a pail. Nobody feeds me. I have to get my own living. I live by my wits. I have to be sharp and clever, lest I go hungry. I have to think things out, catch what I can, take what comes. And it just so happens, my friend, that what comes is flies and insects and bugs. And *further*more," said Charlotte, shaking one of her legs, "do you realize that if I didn't catch bugs and eat them, bugs would increase and multiply and get so numerous that they'd destroy the earth, wipe out everything?"

"Really?" said Wilbur. "I wouldn't want *that* to happen. Perhaps your web is a good thing after all."

The goose had been listening to this conversation and chuckling to herself. "There are a lot of things Wilbur doesn't know about life," she thought. "He's really a very innocent little pig. He doesn't even know what's going to happen to him around Christmastime; he has no idea that Mr Zuckerman and Lurvy are plotting to kill him." And the goose raised herself a bit and poked her eggs a little farther under her so that they would receive the full heat from her warm body and soft feathers.

Charlotte stood quietly over the fly, preparing to eat it. Wilbur lay down and closed his eyes. He was tired from his wakeful night and from the excitement of meeting someone for the first time. A breeze brought him the smell of clover – the sweet-smelling world beyond his fence. "Well," he thought, "I've got a new friend, all right. But what a gamble friendship is! Charlotte is fierce, brutal, scheming, bloodthirsty –

everything I don't like. How can I learn to like her, even though she is pretty and, of course, clever?"

Wilbur was merely suffering the doubts and fears that often go with finding a new friend. In good time he was to discover that he was mistaken about Charlotte. Underneath her rather bold and cruel exterior, she had a kind heart, and she was to prove loyal and true to the very end.

I, HOUDINI

by Lynne Reid Banks

Houdini the hamster has one aim in life – to escape. His adventures take him all over the house: inside the piano, under the floorboards and even up the chimney, leaving a trail of destruction behind him.

Oh, it was wonderful to be free! I scampered down those steps in a twinkling. A feeling of almost hysterical delight came over me as I saw that all the doors downstairs were open. Lights were out – everyone had gone to bed – but it wasn't too dark to see my way, and there were plenty of smells to guide me. I headed for the living room first, the piano room I call it. I was so overjoyed to get back into my piano again! I hadn't realized till then that I had grown – I was now full-size – and to my excitement I found I could now climb right to the top inside. There was a marvellous place there, with rows of little wooden hammer-things, with their tips covered in lovely soft felt.

Ah, I thought. Perfect for a nest! I'd already planned, during my weeks of imprisonment, how I would make nests all over the house to retreat to if I ever got the chance, and stock them with food so that no matter what room I was in I would have a safe refuge, where I could stay for some days.

I got to work on the felts. As soon as I had chewed off enough soft stuff to fill both cheeks, I would nip down to a platform I had found about halfway to the ground, de-cheek the bedding, and then climb up to get more. I did the better part of the whole nest before I allowed myself time off to forage for a bite to eat.

I thought I'd have to go to the kitchen for that, but there was a really delicious smell right there in the living room which I decided to investigate first. I traced it to the area of the fireplace. It was coming down from above somewhere – a fresh, fruity smell, richer and moister than grain. I determined to find out what it was and get some, if it was any good. But how to get up there?

After several head-on attempts which the still-glowing embers foiled, I went to the side of the fireplace. There I found a perfect way up. Mind you, I won't say it was easy. It was a straight wall, with a sticking-out bit covered with rough stuff, like brick or cement; but the wall, luckily for me, was covered with some material like sacking. This gave me all the foothold I needed and, feet spread, I was up that angle as quickly as I went up my tubes at home. Pretty soon I was on the mantelpiece above the fire, and there I found my prize.

It was a large vase full of sprays of red berries. I'd never tasted a berry before, but I had had fresh fruit and salad so I knew it would be good.

I scrambled up the wall, pressing my back against the vase, and pretty soon I was having a marvellous time swinging on the sturdy branches and twigs, scoffing these little red berries until neither my stomach nor my cheeks could hold any more.

I was just turning my thoughts – not without some worries – to the much more difficult downward climb, when I spotted a particularly luscious looking bunch of berries right out on the tip of the branch I was on. Yes, it was sheer greed that made me go for them – I don't deny it. I just couldn't bear to leave them there. Perhaps my antics in the piano and on the stairs had made me too confident. None too cautiously I began to edge along the branch towards the cluster …

Need I go on? With the added weight of the berries in my cheeks, I was too heavy. The branch, the berries, the vase and I were all soon lying in a puddle of water in the hearth, the air around still echoing with the crash the vase made as it broke.

Well, I thought, picking myself up with a dainty shake of my wet fur, at least that solves the problem of getting down. But there was another problem now, because the noise had woken the Father, who could already be heard thumping about upstairs.

Houdini, said I to myself, this is no place for you! Quick as thought, I scurried behind the piano and up into my brand-new nest.

The rows about the telephone wire and the carpet and the door were as nothing compared to what followed my escapade on the mantelpiece. The Father seemed to go completely mad. He literally jumped up and down, purple in the face with rage. (How do I know? I'll tell you. There was a little window in my piano – actually a little sliding-glass panel. Don't ask me why, but it was extremely useful, as I could sit on the hammers in a shadow and peep out at what was going on in the living room. That was where the light came from, inside.) He did more than threaten now – he issued ultimatums.

"Back it goes! That, or I'll kill it – I will – I'll kill it with my bare hands!"

Yes, very intemperate of him, wasn't it? And all that was before he'd discovered – what, needless to say, I had not known – that all that soft stuff I chewed off the little wooden hammers prevented a number of notes from playing on the piano.

He went to the lengths of pulling the piano out from the wall, taking its back off, and hunting for me through all the works. My nest was demolished, of course, and my store of berries was stolen, but fortunately for me, by that time I was no longer there. I had found my favourite place, underneath the kitchen sink.

★ ★ ★

My luck seemed to be in altogether, so far as that kitchen was concerned.

It was not one of your shining modern affairs with all the gadgets, stoves, washing-machines and so forth set so tightly side by side that even a mouse couldn't squeeze between them – no. It was your old-fashioned, half-converted kind, with huge chasms between and behind the bits of equipment. I could safely run right under the stove, for instance, and one of the cabinets – the one which turned out to contain my beloved biscuit drawer – had no back. The drawer itself, three shelves up, was not quite backless, but its back was half broken so that, having swung up to it, it was a simple matter to climb in and help myself. The children's visits to that drawer left it in such chaos that it was a long time before the Mother realized that most of the crumbs, torn wrappings, etc., were my work.

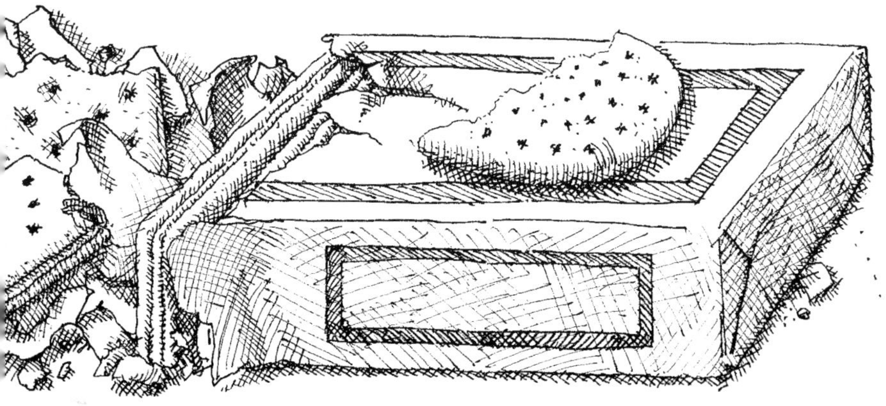

Well! So on my very first exploration of this domestic paradise I discovered, in one corner under the sink, a hole in the floor. You may imagine I was exceedingly careful not to go down into it until I had checked on the distance of the drop below. I soon realized that there was a sort of handy little platform just there, with the real floor about five inches underneath.

The platform had been built to hide a strange tangle of pipes of various kinds which snaked about in the dark under the false floor. They didn't bother me, however. I soon learnt which ones were hot and which weren't, and in fact they provided several cosy little nooks and crannies, in one of which I decided to build my permanent home.

It took labour and planning of course – what dream house doesn't? I lost count of the number of trips I made in the dead of night, carrying all kinds of lovely soft bedding material – carpet fluff, shavings, bits of chewed-up fabrics which I found carelessly left lying about.

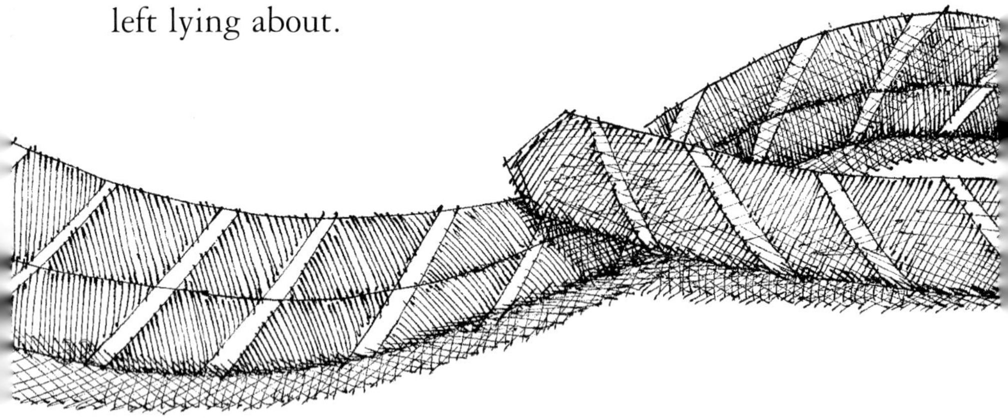

(How could I know that useless-looking stripy thing was Mark's school tie?) Anyway, by the time I had arranged everything to my satisfaction, a number of days had passed and I'm afraid the family had begun to despair of ever seeing me again, because I was very careful to work only after they had gone to bed in order not to draw attention to my activities.

Nobody, I was determined, was going to find this nest – it was the most beautiful I had ever constructed. Nowhere, not even in the piano, had I felt so safe and warm and comfortable. The first night I bedded down there, after feasting from a splendid supply of grain, crumbs and (treat of treats!) raisins that I had found readily available, I felt utterly contented and pleased with myself.

There was just one thing that was not quite perfect. My under-floor home lacked a built-in water supply. When I got thirsty, I had to go out and forage for drink. Sometimes there would be a puddle of water left on the floor near the sink, but I felt lapping up spilt water – often tasting disgustingly of detergent – was beneath my dignity.

The surest source was, of course, my own water bottle in the cage, but that meant going all the way upstairs, slithering back into the opening I had made, having a drink and rushing home again. I could never climb in or out of the cage without making some noise, and I paid for every drink I took in this way in sheer terror that one of the boys would hear me and come out and capture me.

The infuriating thing was, there was water under the platform. In fact, I came to realize that one of the pipes which surrounded my nest was a water pipe. I knew this because there was a joint further along, out of which, when the pressure was high, a few drops of water sometimes leaked. Each time this happened I would think, "How marvellous if there were a tiny hole in the pipe through which I could suck a drink whenever I wanted one!"

This thought preyed on my mind. I would often lie in bed (as you would put it), with comforting rays of light filtering through the cracks in the floorboards, and gaze at that pipe, almost willing it to spring a leak. Needless to say it didn't. Eventually, one hot night, when my thirst was tormenting me and I just didn't feel like climbing mountains and running risks to get water, I decided to do something about it.

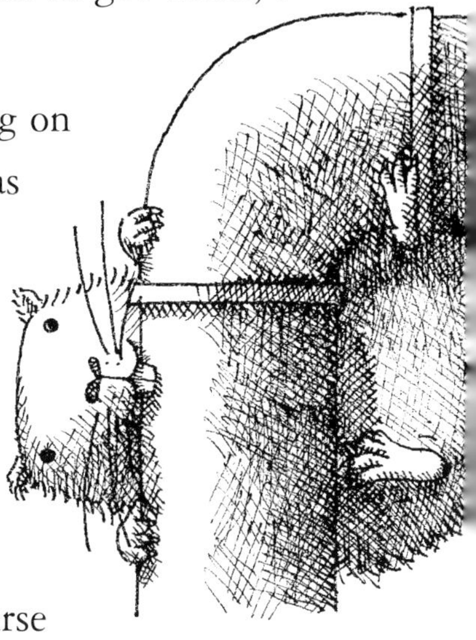

I had long ago learnt that gnawing on metal is useless and painful. That was why I had not had a go at that pipe before. What I now discovered was that not all metals are alike. I thought they were all equally hard and resistant, but as soon as I tried an experimental gnaw, I found that this kind was – well, not soft, of course not, but certainly no harder than a lot of woods.

In fact, I must say that gnawing on this stuff was really very satisfying. If I didn't try to bite it, but just applied my side-teeth to peeling off little threads of it, it came away beautifully. It also wore my teeth down beautifully, so that the process of actually making a hole in the thing took over a week. I didn't want to find myself with stubs instead of teeth.

I made my breakthrough on a Saturday night. I know that because the family usually lie in late on a Sunday, enabling me to be out and about in the morning after my bedtime, foraging for special tidbits for my own Sunday lunch.

On this occasion, though, there was no Sunday lunch for anybody. At dawn, after a night's work, I sensed that I was about to pierce the water pipe. I was belly-deep in fine lead shavings. There was a long, shallow channel of bright, shining metal where I was working, grooved with my tooth marks. I must be nearly there! I could feel the extra coldness of water, right against my lips as I worked. Just one more good gnaw–

Whoosh!

The next second I was flat on my back. A jet of water, which had hit me in the face and bowled me over, was making a swift-running stream across the floor. My lovely nest was awash, my fur soaked. I jumped up and fled into a far corner, out of the way of the stream, which rapidly enlarged into a river. The water as it came out of the pipe made a hissing noise every bit as sinister as the hiss of an enraged hamster. For my part, I was dumb with horror. What, oh what had I done?

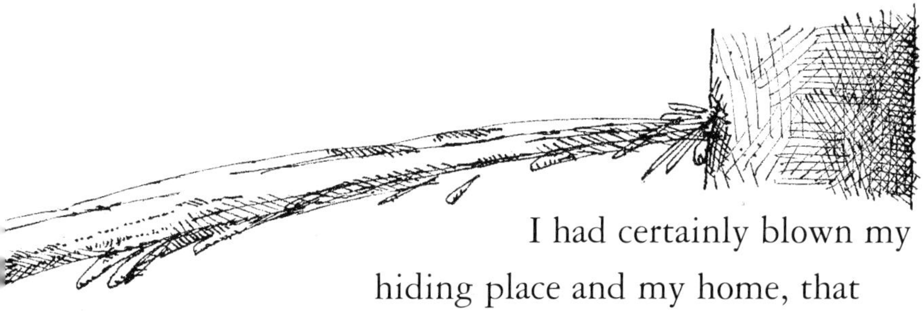

I had certainly blown my hiding place and my home, that was sure. I decided that discretion, as they say, was the better part of valour. I waded across the river, which was now flowing out from under the platform over the rest of the kitchen floor, came up through my entrance hole, took one appalled look at the spreading lake, and ran as fast as my little legs would carry me to the safest place I could think of. My cage. Foolishly no doubt, I thought that if I were found there, a self-surrendered captive, suspicion would not fall on me.

I cowered in my loft, wondering what was happening downstairs and willing someone to go down and stop the water before the whole house was flooded. At the same time I hoped they never would, for I could not imagine what sort of row would follow. Perhaps I wouldn't be blamed? I had all too little hope. The Father had become quite neurotic about me, blaming me for everything that went wrong in the house, including the loss of his hammer and the disappearance (later traced to Guy) of a two-pound box of after dinner mints. As if I'd be caught dead eating anything so bad for my teeth! (Well, except on festive occasions!)

At last Mark got up and padded sleepily downstairs to get something to eat. I crouched with closed eyes, every nerve alert for the outcry. It came, shatteringly.

"MUMMY! DADDY! The kitchen's flooded!"

A moment later he came flying up the stairs, his face alight with excitement and delight.

I cowered down in the musty old bedding I hadn't used for weeks. The loft roof overhead was clear, and as the Mother and Father, roused from their Sunday lie-in, came pelting along the corridor. I felt as if the ceiling were about to fall on me. What a fool I'd been to go to my cage! What a simpleton!

The whole family thundered past me and down the stairs like a herd of elephants, and I crouched, waiting for the explosion. Of course you'll say I should have wriggled out and fled to a secure hiding place straight away, but the shameful truth was, I was too terrified to move. I heard the Father give voice to a bellow of dismay, while everyone else uttered shrieks and cries and exclamations and questions that went on for about ten minutes. It seemed like ten hours to me. I expected every second that they would come thundering up again, and rend me limb from limb, but to my great relief, nothing of the sort happened.

Slowly everything quietened down. After a bit, the boys were sent upstairs to dry their feet (I assumed they'd been paddling) and get dressed. As Adam went past the cage he suddenly stopped dead.

"Look!" he cried in wonder. "It's Houdini! He's back!"

I opened one eye just long enough to see they were all crouching round me, and then I pretended to be asleep. There was such a long silence, though, that I had another peep to see why they weren't talking. The reason was, they were all looking at each other and then at me. When they did speak, it was in whispers.

"Why would he go back in by himself?"

"Unless he had a guilty conscience!"

"What's that?" hissed Guy. (It was the first time I'd heard the expression, but I knew what it meant all right!)

"He knows he did something awful, Dumbo!" Mark hissed back. "And we know what it was!"

"But we mustn't tell!" Adam said, forgetting to whisper. Mark bowled him over backwards and sat on his head.

"SHHHH! If Dad ever finds out it was him ..."

"If we guessed, he will too!" croaked Adam from underneath Mark.

"Then we'll take Houdini out of there and hide him somewhere else till the trouble blows over."

And that, friends, is how I found myself back in that thrice-accursed bin.

With the lid on.

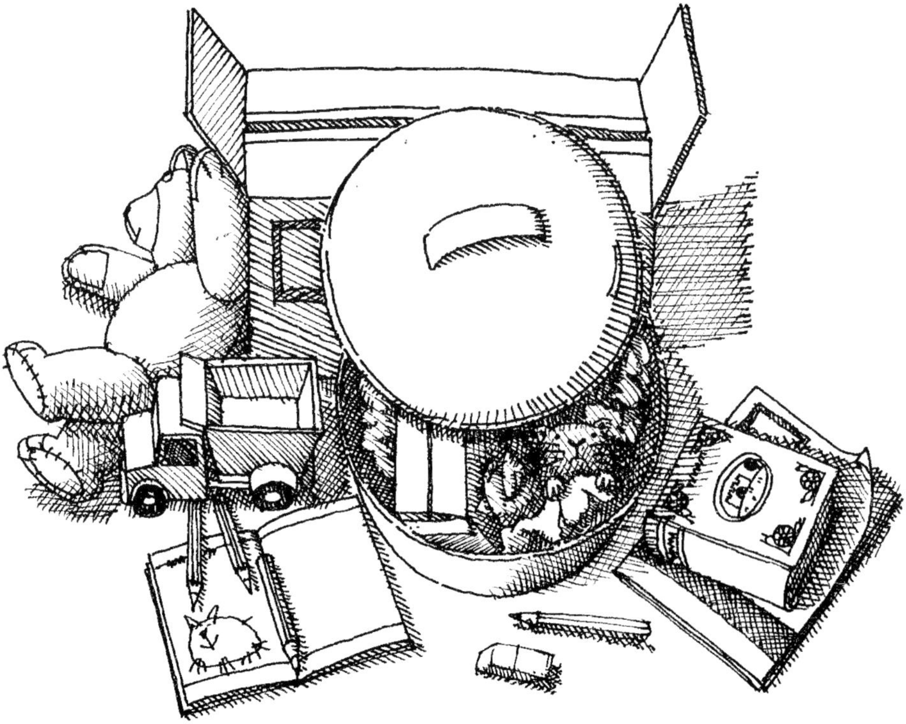

Toomai of the Elephants

by Rudyard Kipling

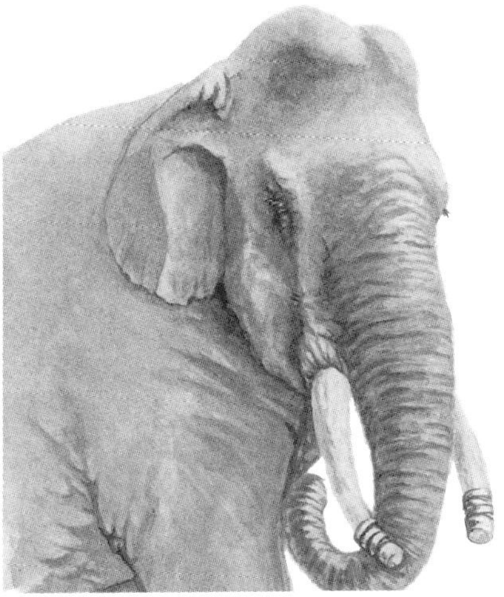

The mighty elephant Kala Nag (whose name means "Black Snake") was at least 70 years old, huge, strong, brave, clever and absolutely trustworthy. He worked in the service of the Indian Government, helping to catch and train wild elephants from the jungle. Little Toomai was only a boy, but, like his father and grandfather, he lived and worked with Kala Nag, who obeyed and loved him. When the Keddah (elephant hunt) was over, and the elephant hunters finally left the jungle and took the elephants they had caught down to the plains, it was believed that the elephants who had escaped capture celebrated with a dance. But it was only a story. No one had ever seen it happen. Until one night …

Little Toomai felt sleepy and stretched himself on the fodder at Kala Nag's side. At last the elephants began to lie down one after another as is their custom, till only Kala Nag at the right of the line was left standing up; and he rocked slowly from side to side, his ears put forward to listen to the night wind as it blew very slowly across the hills. The air was full of all the night noises that, taken together, make one big silence – the click of one bamboo stem against the other, the rustle of something alive in the undergrowth, the scratch and squawk of a half-waked bird (birds are awake in the night much more often than we imagine), and the fall of water ever so far away.

Little Toomai slept for some time. When he waked it was brilliant moonlight, and Kala Nag was still standing up with his ears cocked. Little Toomai turned, rustling in the fodder, and watched the curve of his big back against half the stars in heaven, and while he watched he heard, so far away that it sounded no more than a pinhole of noise pricked through the stillness, the "hoot-toot" of a wild elephant.

All the elephants in the lines jumped up as if they had been shot. Their grunts at last waked the sleeping mahouts, and they came out and drove in the picket pegs with big mallets, and tightened this rope and knotted that, till all was quiet. One new elephant had nearly grubbed up his picket, and Big Toomai took off Kala Nag's leg chain and shackled that elephant fore-foot to hind-foot, but slipped a loop of grass string round Kala Nag's leg, and told him to remember that he was tied fast. He knew that he and his father and his grandfather had done the very same thing hundreds of times before. Kala Nag did not answer to the order by gurgling, as he usually did. He stood still, looking out across the moonlight, his head a little raised and his ears spread like fans, up to the great folds of the Garo hills.

"Tend to him if he grows restless in the night," said Big Toomai to Little Toomai, and he went into the hut and slept. Little Toomai was just going to sleep, too, when he heard the coir string snap with a little "tang", and Kala Nag rolled out of his pickets as slowly and as silently as a cloud rolls out of the mouth of a valley. Little Toomai pattered after him, barefooted, down the road in the moonlight, calling under his breath, "Kala Nag! Kala Nag! Take me with you, O Kala Nag!" The elephant turned, without a sound, took three strides back to the boy in the moonlight, put down his trunk, swung him up to his neck, and almost before Little Toomai had settled his knees, slipped into the forest.

There was one blast of furious trumpeting from the lines, and then the silence shut down on everything, and Kala Nag began to move. Sometimes a tuft of high grass washed along his sides as a wave washes along the sides of a ship, and sometimes a cluster of wild-pepper vines would scrape along his back, or a bamboo would creak where his shoulder touched it. But between those times he moved absolutely without any sound, drifting through the thick Garo forest as though it had been smoke. He was going uphill, but though Little Toomai watched the stars in the rifts of the trees, he could not tell in what direction.

Kala Nag reached the crest of the ascent and stopped for a minute, and Little Toomai could see the tops of the trees lying all speckled and furry under the moonlight for miles and miles, and the blue-white mist over the river in the hollow. Toomai leaned forward and looked, and he felt that the forest was awake

below him – awake and alive and crowded. A big brown fruit-eating bat brushed past his ear; a porcupine's quills rattled in the thicket; and in the darkness between the tree stems he heard a hog-bear digging hard in the moist warm earth, and snuffing as it dug.

Then the branches closed over his head again, and Kala Nag began to go down into the valley – not quietly this time, but as a runaway gun goes down a steep bank – in one rush. The huge limbs moved as steadily as pistons, eight feet to each stride, and the wrinkled skin of the elbow points rustled. The undergrowth on either side of him ripped with a noise like torn canvas, and the saplings that he heaved away right and left with his shoulders sprang back again and banged him on the flank, and great trails of creepers, all matted together, hung from his tusks as he threw his head from side to side and ploughed out his pathway.

Then Little Toomai laid himself down close to the great neck lest a swinging bough should sweep him to the ground, and he wished that he were back in the lines again.

The grass began to get squashy, and Kala Nag's feet sucked and squelched as he put them down, and the night mist at the bottom of the valley chilled Little Toomai. There was a splash and a trample, and the rush of running water, and Kala Nag strode through the bed of a river, feeling his way at each step. Above the noise of the water, as it swirled round the elephant's legs, Little Toomai could hear more splashing and some trumpeting both upstream and down – great grunts and angry snortings, and all the mist about him seemed to be full of rolling, wavy shadows.

"Ai!" he said, half aloud, his teeth chattering. "The elephant-folk are out tonight. It is the dance, then!"

Kala Nag swashed out of the water, blew his trunk clear, and began another climb. This time he was not alone, and he had not to make his path. That was made already, six feet wide, in front of him, where the bent jungle-grass was trying to recover itself and stand up.

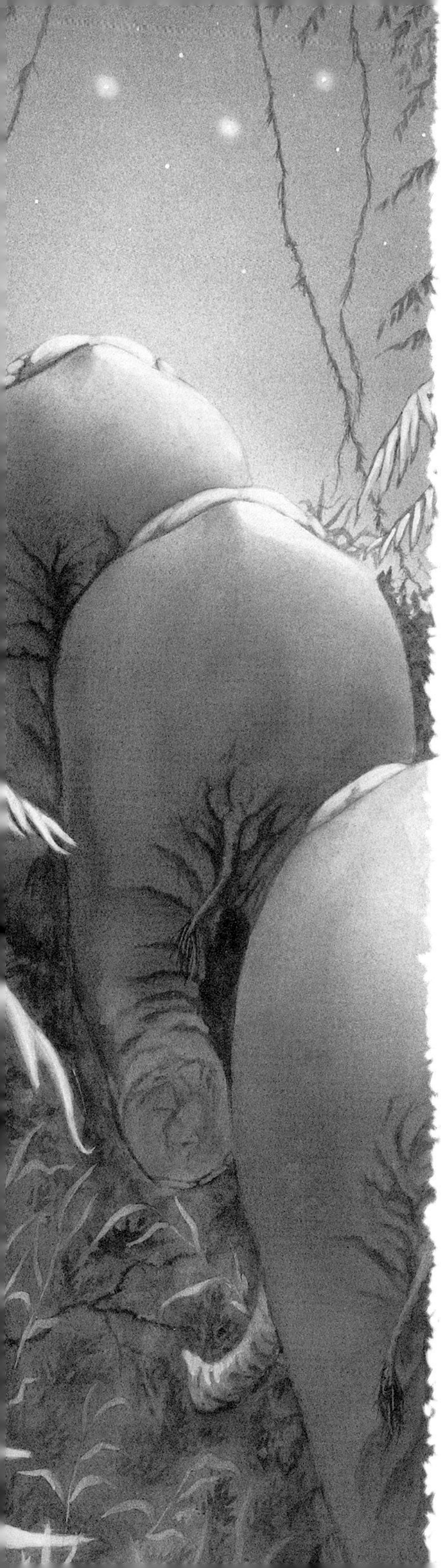

Many elephants must have gone that way only a few minutes before. Little Toomai looked back, and behind him a great wild tusker with his little pig's eyes glowing like hot coals was just lifting himself out of the misty river. Then the trees closed up again, and they went on and up, with trumpetings and crashings, and the sound of breaking branches on every side of them.

At last Kala Nag stood still between two tree-trunks at the very top of the hill. They were part of a circle of trees that grew round an irregular space of some three or four acres, and in all that space, as Little Toomai could see, the ground had been trampled down as hard as a brick floor. Some trees grew in the centre of the clearing, but their bark was rubbed away, and the white wood beneath showed all shiny and polished in the patches of moonlight. There were creepers hanging from the upper branches, and the bells of the flowers of the creepers, great waxy white things like convolvuluses, hung down fast asleep. But within the limits of the clearing there was not a single blade of green – nothing but the trampled earth.

The moonlight showed it all iron grey, except where some elephants stood upon it, and their shadows were inky black. Little Toomai looked, holding his breath, with his eyes starting out of his head, and as he looked, more and more and more elephants swung out into the open from between the tree trunks. Little Toomai could only count up to ten, and he counted again and again on his fingers till he lost count of the tens, and his head began to swim. Outside the clearing he could hear them crashing in the undergrowth as they worked their way up the hillside, but as soon as they were within the circle of the tree trunks they moved like ghosts.

There were white-tusked wild males, with fallen leaves and nuts and twigs lying in the wrinkles of their necks and the folds of their ears; fat, slow-footed she-elephants, with restless little pinky-black calves, only three or four feet high running under their stomachs; young elephants with their tusks just beginning to show, and very proud of them; lanky, scraggy old-maid

elephants, with their hollow anxious faces, and trunks like rough bark; savage old bull elephants, scarred from shoulder to flank with great weals and cuts of bygone fights, and the caked dirt of their solitary mud baths dropping from their shoulders; and there was one with a broken tusk and the marks of the full-stroke, the terrible drawing scrape, of a tiger's claws on his side.

They were standing head to head, or walking to and fro across the ground in couples, or rocking and swaying all by themselves – scores and scores of elephants.

Toomai knew that so long as he lay still on Kala Nag's neck nothing would happen to him, for even in the rush and scramble of a Keddah drive a wild elephant does not reach up with his trunk and drag a man off the neck of a tame elephant. And these elephants were not thinking of men that night. Once they started and put their ears forward when they heard the chinking of a leg iron in the forest, but it was Pudmini, Petersen Sahib's pet elephant, her chain snapped short off, grunting, snuffling up the hillside. She must have broken her pickets and come straight from Petersen Sahib's camp; and Little Toomai saw another elephant, one that he did not know, with deep rope galls on his back and breast. He, too, must have run away from some camp in the hills about.

At last there was no sound of any more elephants moving in the forest, and Kala Nag rolled out from his station between the trees and went into the middle of the crowd, clucking and gurgling, and all the elephants began to talk in their own tongue, and to move about.

Still lying down, Little Toomai looked down upon scores and scores of broad backs, and wagging ears, and tossing trunks, and little rolling eyes. He heard the click of tusks as they crossed other tusks by accident, and the dry rustle of trunks twined together, and the chafing

of enormous sides and shoulders in the crowd, and the incessant flick and hiss of the great tails. Then a cloud came over the moon, and he sat in black darkness, but the quiet, steady hustling and pushing and gurgling went on just the same. He knew that there were elephants all round Kala Nag, and that there was no chance of backing him out of the assembly; so he set his teeth and shivered. In a Keddah at least there was torchlight and shouting, but here he was all alone in the dark, and once a trunk came up and touched him on the knee.

Then an elephant trumpeted, and they all took it up for five or ten terrible seconds. The dew from the trees above spattered down like rain on the unseen backs, and a dull booming noise began, not very loud at first, and Little Toomai could not tell what it was. It grew and grew, and Kala Nag lifted up one forefoot and then the other, and brought them down on the ground – one-two, one-two, as steadily as trip-hammers. The elephants were stamping all together now, and it sounded like a war drum beaten at the mouth of a cave. The dew fell from the trees till there was no more left to fall, and the booming went on, and the ground rocked and shivered, and Little Toomai put his hands up to his ears to shut out the sound. But it was all one gigantic jar that ran through him – this stamp of hundreds of heavy feet on the raw earth. Once or twice he could feel Kala Nag and all the others surge forward a few strides, and the thumping would change to the crushing sound of juicy green things being bruised; but in a minute or two the boom of feet on hard earth began again.

A tree was creaking and groaning somewhere near him. He put out his arm and felt the bark, but Kala Nag moved forward, still tramping, and he could not tell where he was in the clearing.

There was no sound from the elephants, except once, when two or three little calves squeaked together. Then he heard a thump and a shuffle, and the booming went on. It must have lasted fully two hours, and Little Toomai ached in every nerve, but he knew by the smell of the night air that the dawn was coming.

The morning broke in one sheet of pale yellow behind the green hills, and the booming stopped with the first ray, as though the light had been an order. Before Little Toomai had got the ringing out of his head, before even he had shifted his position, there was not an elephant in sight except Kala Nag, Pudmini, and the elephant with the rope-galls, and there was neither sign nor rustle nor whisper down the hillsides to show where the others had gone.

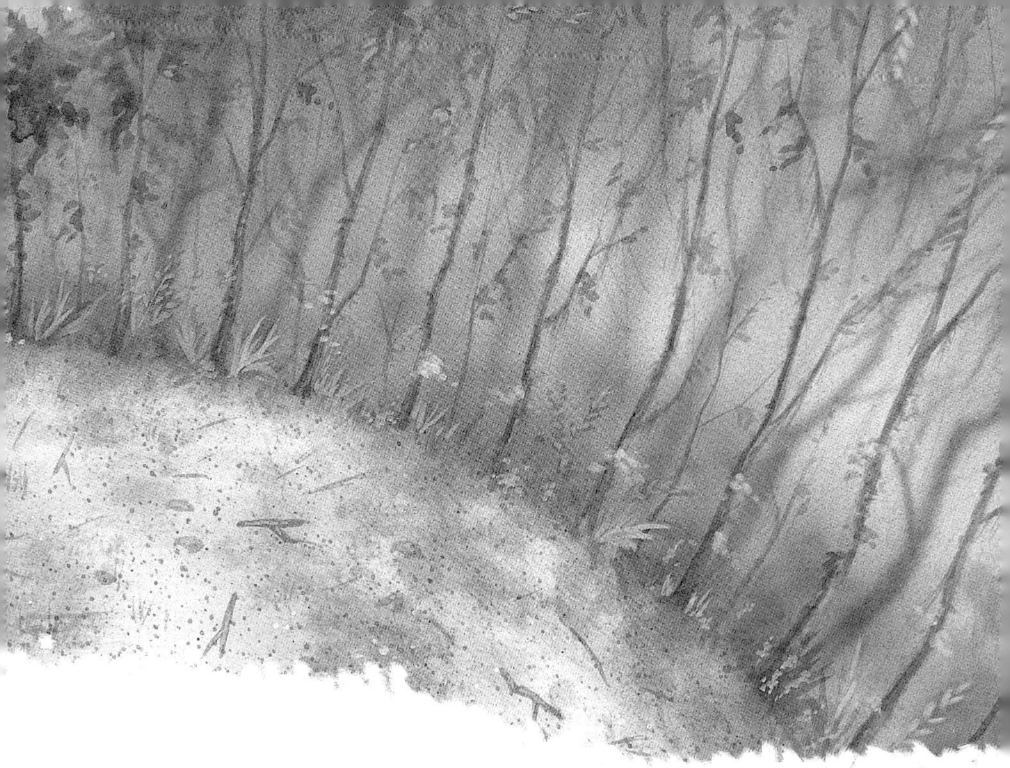

Little Toomai stared again and again. The clearing, as he remembered it, had grown in the night. More trees stood in the middle of it, but the undergrowth and the jungle grass at the sides had been rolled back. Little Toomai stared once more. Now he understood the trampling. The elephants had stamped out more room – had stamped the thick grass and juicy cane to trash, the trash into slivers, the slivers into tiny fibres, and the fibres into hard earth.

"Wah!" said Little Toomai, and his eyes were very heavy. "Kala Nag, my lord, let us keep by Pudmini and go to Petersen Sahib's camp, or I shall drop from thy neck."

The third elephant watched the two go away, snorted, wheeled round, and took his own path. He may have belonged to some little native king's establishment, fifty or sixty or a hundred miles away.

Two hours later, as Petersen Sahib was eating early breakfast, his elephants, who had been double chained that night, began to trumpet, and Pudmini, mired to the shoulders, with Kala Nag, very footsore, shambled into the camp. Little Toomai's face was grey and pinched, and his hair was full of leaves and drenched with dew, but he tried to salute Petersen Sahib, and cried faintly: "The dance – the elephant dance! I have seen it, and – I die!" As Kala Nag sat down, he slid off his neck in a dead faint.

But, since native children have no nerves worth speaking of, in two hours he was lying very contentedly in Petersen Sahib's hammock with Petersen Sahib's shooting-coat under his head, and a glass of warm milk, a little brandy, with a dash of quinine, inside of him, and while the old hairy, scarred hunters of the jungles sat three deep before him, looking at him as though he were a spirit, he told his tale in short words, as a child will, and wound up with:

"Now, if I lie in one word, send men to see, and they will find that the elephant folk have trampled down more room in their dance-room, and they will find ten and ten, and many times ten, tracks leading to that dance-room. They made more room with their feet. I have seen it. Kala Nag took me, and I saw. Also Kala Nag is very leg-weary!"

Little Toomai lay back and slept all through the long afternoon and into the twilight, and while he slept Petersen Sahib and Machua Appa followed the track of the two elephants for fifteen miles across the hills. Petersen Sahib had spent eighteen years in catching elephants, and he had only once before found such a dance-place. Machua Appa had no need to look twice at the clearing to see what had been done there, or to scratch with his toe in the packed, rammed earth.

"The child speaks truth," said he. "All this was done last night, and I have counted seventy tracks crossing the river. See, Sahib, where Pudmini's leg-iron cut the bark of that tree! Yes; she was there too."

They looked at one another and up and down, and they wondered. For the ways of elephants are beyond the wit of any man, black or white, to fathom.

"Forty years and five," said Machua Appa, "have I followed my lord, the elephant, but never have I heard that any child of man had seen what this child has seen."

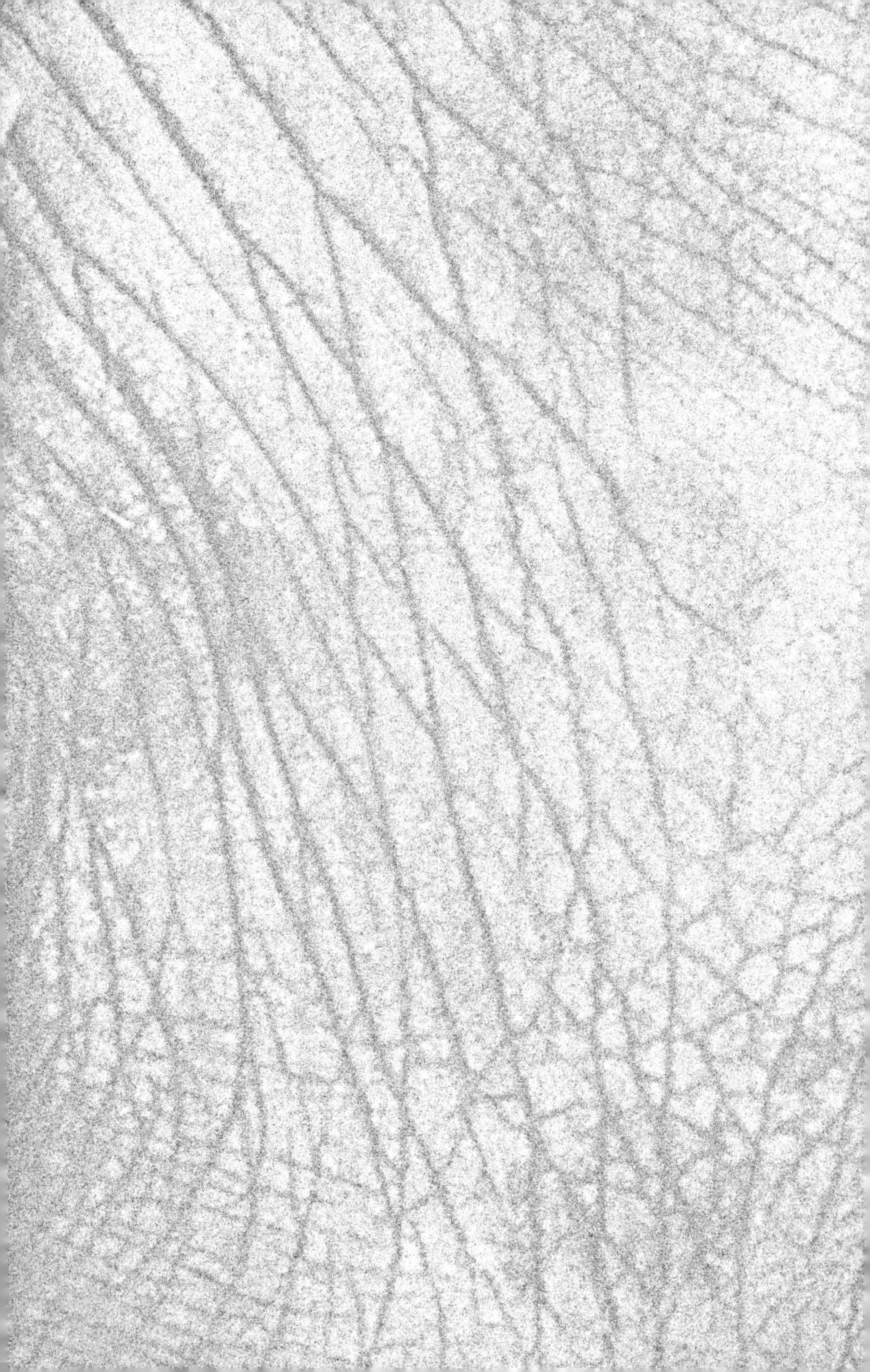